PIANO ★ VOCAL ★ CHORDS

RAGTIME
VOCAL SELECTIONS

WARNER BROS. PUBLICATIONS - THE GLOBAL LEADER IN PRINT
USA: 15800 NW 48th Avenue, Miami, FL 33014

WARNER/CHAPPELL MUSIC
CANADA: 85 SCARSDALE ROAD, SUITE 101
DON MILLS, ONTARIO, M3B 2R2
SCANDINAVIA: P.O. BOX 533, VENDEVAGEN 85 B
S-182 15, DANDERYD, SWEDEN
AUSTRALIA: P.O. BOX 353
3 TALAVERA ROAD, NORTH RYDE N.S.W. 2113

Carisch
NUOVA CARISCH
ITALY: VIA M.F. QUINTILIANO 40
20138 MILANO
SPAIN: MAGALLANES, 25
28015 MADRID

IMP
INTERNATIONAL MUSIC PUBLICATIONS LIMITED
ENGLAND: SOUTHEND ROAD,
WCODFORD GREEN, ESSEX IG8 8HN
FRANCE: 25 RUE DE HAUTEVILLE, 75010 PARIS
GERMANY: MARSTALLISTR. 8, D-80539 MUNCHEN
DENMARK: DANMUSIK, VOGNMAGERGADE 7
DK 1120 KOBENHAVNK

PROJECT MANAGER: SY FELDMAN
BOOK LAYOUT: KEN REHM

LIVENT INC.

presents

BRIAN STOKES MITCHELL   PETER FRIEDMAN   MARIN MAZZIE
AUDRA McDONALD   MARK JACOBY

in

RAGTIME

Book by
TERRENCE McNALLY

Music by
STEPHEN FLAHERTY

Lyrics by
LYNN AHRENS

Based on the novel by **E.L. DOCTOROW**

featuring

RICHARD ALLEN   JIM CORTI   LYNETTE PERRY   STEVEN SUTCLIFFE

and **CAMILLE SAVIOLA** as "Emma Goldman"

with

LARRY DAGGETT   DAVID MUCCI   MIKE O'CARROLL   PAUL SOLES   VANESSA TOWNSELL-CRISP
PAUL FRANKLIN DANO   LEA MICHELE

Production Design by
EUGENE LEE

Costume Design by
SANTO LOQUASTO

Sound Design by
JONATHAN DEANS

Lighting Design by
JULES FISHER and
PEGGY EISENHAUER

Orchestrations by
WILLIAM DAVID BROHN

Music Supervisor/Conductor
JEFFREY HUARD

Dance Music Arranged by
DAVID KRANE

Vocal Arrangements by
STEPHEN FLAHERTY

Video & Projections Designed by
JOHN BOESCHE

Magic Illusions by
FRANZ HARARY

Associate Choreographer
WILLIE ROSARIO

Casting by
BETH RUSSELL and
ARNOLD J. MUNGIOLI, C.S.A.

Musical Staging by
GRACIELA DANIELE

Directed by
FRANK GALATI

World Premiere Recording "Songs from *Ragtime, The Musical*"
available in the United States from RCA Victor
and in Canada from BMG Music Canada.
All production photos are of the original Toronto cast.

A vaudeville re-enactment of the trial of Evelyn Nesbit's husband, Harry K. Thaw, in the murder of celebrated architect, Stanford White. Lynnette Perry (on the swing) as Evelyn Nesbit and the "Ragtime" Ensemble.

On the dock of New York Harbor. (Left to Right) Jeffrey Kuhn, Jamie Chandler-Torns,
Paul Franklin Dano as the Little Boy, Marin Mazzie as Mother, Mark Jacoby as Father, Steven Sutcliffe as Mother's Younger Brother, Paul Soles as Grandfather and "Ragtime" Ensemble.

Coalhouse Walker Jr.'s vision of workers in Henry Ford's auto assembly factory. Brian Stokes Mitchell and the "Ragtime" Ensemble.

RAGTIME THE STORY: ACT ONE

New Rochelle, New York, 1906. A large Victorian house on Broadview Avenue, the home of an upper middle class family: Father, who has derived his wealth from the manufacture of fireworks, flags and bunting; Mother; their son, the Little Boy; and Mother's Younger Brother, a genius at explosives who works in Father's fireworks factory. This is the Gilded Age, an era of industrialization, when prospects for wealth and happiness seem to be boundless. Everything is new and anything is possible.

In Harlem, crowds dance to the music of ragtime pianist Coalhouse Walker Jr. In Latvia, a widower named Tateh dreams of escaping with his daughter, the Little Girl, to America.

America is filled with famous characters: mesmerizing illusionist and escape artist Harry Houdini ... J.P. Morgan, the wealthiest man in America ... radical anarchist Emma Goldman ... chorus girl Evelyn Nesbit, former mistress of Stanford White, the brilliant architect who has been slain by Nesbit's millionaire husband, Harry K. Thaw. Called the "Crime of the Century," this murder has scandalized the nation (**Ragtime**).

On the dock of New York Harbor, Mother bids farewell to Father who is joining Admiral Peary on an expedition to the North Pole (**Goodbye, My Love**). As the boat disappears into the distance, another appears. It is a rag ship sailing to America, carrying refugees from western and eastern Europe, including Tateh and the Little Girl.

Infatuated with Evelyn Nesbit, Younger Brother visits a vaudeville house in Manhattan every night to see her perform. One night, a news photographer waits for Evelyn. She kisses Younger Brother merely for the publicity, then saunters away, leaving Younger Brother heartbroken and disillusioned.

In New Rochelle, Mother, who is planting in her garden, is shocked when she finds a black infant boy. The police arrive with Sarah, the scared and mute mother of the child. Before the police can charge Sarah with attempted murder, Mother intervenes, saying she will take responsibility for Sarah and her baby. Mother brings them into her home.

On Ellis Island, crowds of immigrants, including Tateh and the Little Girl, arrive, delirious with joy and optimism. On the streets of the Lower East Side of Manhattan, Tateh calls out from his cart to passersby, offering to sell them paper silhouette portraits, with very little success. Months pass. Tateh's desperation increases. A man stops, but instead of buying a silhouette, he asks Tateh to sell him the Little Girl. Enraged, Tateh attacks the man. Full of self doubt, Tateh wonders whether America's golden promise was only a lie. In his disillusionment, he has a vision of Harry Houdini. Tateh is inspired to escape his own confining circumstances. He sells his cart and, with the Little Girl, leaves New York on a trolley. The little money he has will take them as far as Boston.

In the Tempo Nightclub in Harlem, Coalhouse Walker Jr. entertains the crowd. While introducing one of his numbers, he reminisces about a woman he loved named Sarah, and vows to win her back.

Henry Ford and his assembly line appear before Coalhouse in an apparition and he watches intently while a Model T is built. This is the new mass production technology that will transform the country and the world. Coalhouse buys one of these new cars.

In New Rochelle, Coalhouse asks firemen outside the Emerald Isle firehouse for directions to Broadview Avenue. Chief Willie Conklin forbids Coalhouse to pass and forces him to turn back. In the house on Broadview Avenue, Sarah sings a lullaby to her child (**Your Daddy's Son**). Coalhouse arrives and asks to speak with Sarah. Sarah refuses to see him. Coalhouse leaves, but persistently returns every Sunday for several weeks, hoping Sarah will speak with him. Finally, Mother invites Coalhouse in for tea. Coalhouse tells Mother he is a musician, and she invites him to play a tune on the piano. Coalhouse obliges, playing a ragtime melody.

Five months pass. One Sunday, Father returns home unannounced from the North Pole. Surprised to see Sarah, her baby and Coalhouse in his house and to learn about Sarah's predicament, Father wonders whether he has been away too long. Mother ponders why they have grown apart, and are unable to experience the love that Coalhouse has for Sarah, a sentiment shared by Younger Brother. Sarah finally heeds Coalhouse's words of love and comes downstairs into his embrace (**New Music**). Coalhouse takes Sarah and their baby for a ride in his new Model T. Coalhouse promises Sarah that this is the beginning of a new life and a better time for them and their son (**Wheels Of A Dream**).

In Lawrence, Massachusetts, Tateh works in front of a loom for 64 hours a week for just under six dollars. One day, the workers go on strike. In New York, at a rally at a workmen's hall in Union Square, Younger Brother hears Emma Goldman call for a general strike in support of the striking mill workers. Inspired by her passionate words, Younger Brother calls out his support. Within three days, every mill in Lawrence is shut down. Factory owners call in the militia to protect their property. Tateh puts the Little Girl on a train that will take her to a home for safety. A riot breaks out. Tateh hears the panic stricken cries of his daughter as the train begins to move. Tateh runs and ultimately pulls himself onto the train. He comforts the Little Girl with a flip book of silhouette images of her skating that move as he flicks the pages (**Gliding**). A Conductor is attracted by the moving picture book and buys it.

In New Rochelle, Coalhouse and Sarah drive by the Emerald Isle firehouse. Again, Willie Conklin and the firemen block their way. Willie speaks abusively to Coalhouse, demanding twenty-five dollars, claiming that Coalhouse is driving on a private toll road. Wanting to confront the firemen on his own, Coalhouse orders Sarah to leave. Coalhouse leaves the car to look for a policeman. The firemen vandalize and destroy the car. Coalhouse returns. Seeing what they have done, he vows to find justice. Increasingly frustrated and outraged by bureaucratic apathy and ineptitude and the law's delay, Coalhouse proclaims he will not marry until his property is restored to him. Sarah is shattered, but she is determined to help Coalhouse. At a political rally, she attempts to speak with the Republican vice-presidential candidate. The police, thinking Sarah is armed, club her with their nightsticks. She dies. Coalhouse, Mother, Younger Brother, Tateh, Emma Goldman and Sarah's friends mourn her death (**'Till We Reach That Day**).

ACT TWO

In New Rochelle's Main Street Theatre, Harry Houdini is handcuffed inside a packing case. Willie Conklin and his firemen then place the Little Boy and a package of dynamite inside with him. The firemen nail the case shut and it is lifted above the stage. The case explodes in mid-air and falls open. It is empty. Suddenly, in his bed in the house on Broadview Avenue, the

"Ragtime" Ensemble

Little Boy sits up, wide awake. Houdini's escape was a nightmare, and the Little Boy senses that many people are about to die.

Coalhouse has begun a reign of vengeance and terror, killing firemen and burning down firehouses. Coalhouse declares he will agree to end the violence when his car is restored to him in its original condition and Willie Conklin is turned over to him.

In New Rochelle, reporters and photographers descend upon the house, searching for information about Coalhouse. Tension grips Mother, Father and Younger Brother. Father chides Mother for taking Sarah in, blaming her "foolish female sentimentality." Younger Brother defends Coalhouse and attacks Father for his complacency. Younger Brother angrily leaves.

To relieve the pressure, Father takes the child to a baseball game. Father's expectations of a civilized afternoon are disrupted by the rowdy behavior of the many immigrants and lower class people in the crowd.

Back home, reporters continue to besiege Father and his family. Father suggests that the family take a trip to Atlantic City to escape the harassment.

On Atlantic City's boardwalk, elegant vacationers are filmed by the Baron Ashkenazy, a director. The Baron introduces himself to Mother and her family and tells them about his career in the new motion picture industry (**Buffalo Nickel Photoplay, Inc.**).

As evening falls, Evelyn Nesbit and Harry Houdini stroll on the boardwalk and meet. Disillusioned, they commiserate about how fast the world is changing and how fleeting their fame is.

The next morning, Mother and the Baron chat while his daughter and the Little Boy play together. Mother is attracted by the Baron's charm; he is drawn to her kindness. The Baron confides that he is not really a Baron. He is Tateh, a poor immigrant Jew who wants to give his daughter a better future. Mother is moved, and says she is happy their children are friends (**Our Children**).

In Harlem, Younger Brother searches the streets for Coalhouse, but he is greeted with derision and told to leave. He meets one of Coalhouse's followers who takes him to their hideout. As they

depart, Coalhouse emerges from the shadows. Seeing two lovers on the street, Coalhouse reminisces about the first time he met Sarah (**Sarah Brown Eyes**). Younger Brother arrives at the hideout, blindfolded. Coalhouse allows Younger Brother to join him and his men, vowing that with Younger Brother's genius and dynamite, he will unleash an act so terrible that no white man will ever mistreat a black person again.

In Atlantic City, Father tells Mother he has been called back to New York City--Coalhouse and his men have taken over the Morgan Library and threatened to blow up the building and its priceless contents unless his demands are met by that evening. The authorities believe Father, as someone who knows Coalhouse, can help them negotiate a peaceful settlement. Father promises Mother that when this crisis is over, their lives will be as they were before Mother found Coalhouse and Sarah's baby, that they will once again be happy. Mother tells him things will never be the same (**Back To Before**).

In New York, a crowd of police, reporters and onlookers maintains a vigil outside of the library. Willie Conklin is restoring Coalhouse's car, but the authorities refuse to hand the fire chief over to the ragtime musician. They demand that Coalhouse come out of the library. Father arrives and tells them Coalhouse will listen to Booker T. Washington.

Coalhouse sits inside the library surrounded by many priceless treasures and artworks. Bundles of dynamite are everywhere. Among his men is Younger Brother. Booker T. Washington enters. Coalhouse respectfully tells Washington he always tried to follow Washington's words of wisdom and action. Washington replies that Coalhouse's actions are the destruction of everything for which he has fought. Washington, reminding Coalhouse about the legacy he will leave his son, urges him to give up and leave the library, promising that he will intercede on Coalhouse's behalf during his trial. Despite angry protests from his men, Coalhouse agrees to surrender on the condition that his men can leave unharmed. Washington departs.

A hostage arrives at the door. It is Father. Recognizing Younger Brother, Father angrily tells him he owes his sister, Mother, an explanation. Younger Brother asks Father to tell Mother that he has always loved and admired her. Father tells Coalhouse that his restored car is ready. As he prepares to leave, Coalhouse urges his men to tell their story to ensure his struggle was not in vain (**Make Them Hear You**).

Coalhouse's men leave the museum and drive off. Assured that his men are safe, Coalhouse thanks Father for his family's kindness and prepares to leave. Coalhouse asks Father whether he will be killed. Father replies "No," that the authorities are decent men. Coalhouse walks out the door and is greeted by a barrage of gunfire.

Following Coalhouse's death, Younger Brother joins the great peasant revolutionary Emiliano Zapata in Mexico. In Sarajevo in 1914, Archduke Franz Ferdinand is assassinated, triggering World War I. In the Atlantic in 1915, Father is among the 1,200 men, women and children who perish when the Lusitania is torpedoed by a U boat off the Southwest coast of Ireland. After mourning for a year, Mother accepts a marriage proposal from Tateh whom she adores. Together with the Little Boy, the Little Girl, and Coalhouse and Sarah's son, also named Coalhouse, they move to California to make a new home and start a new life (**Ragtime Reprise**).

*The era of Ragtime has run out...as if history were no more than a tune on a player piano.**

The Tempo Club

*by E.L. Doctorow
RAGTIME, 1975

Synopsis by Dennis Kucherawy

Richard Allen as Booker T. Washington (left), Brian Stokes Mitchell as Coalhouse Walker Jr. (right) and Emerald Isle firemen in New Rochelle, New York.

In search of justice, Sarah attempts to speak with the Republican vice-presidential candidate at Pennsylvania Station in New York City. Audra McDonald as Sarah and the "Ragtime" Ensemble.

Emma Goldman addresses a rally at a workmen's hall in Union Square in New York City. Camille Saviola as Emma Goldman (center left), Steven Sutcliffe as Younger Brother (center right) and the "Ragtime" Ensemble.

Immigrants arrive at Ellis Island. Lea Michele as the Little Girl (center left) and Peter Friedman as Tateh (center right) and the "Ragtime" Ensemble.

ABOUT THE COMPOSERS

LYNN AHRENS (Lyrics) and **STEPHEN FLAHERTY** (Music) are Broadway's new generation, a songwriting team in the tradition of the American musical theatre's finest collaborations.

Their most current achievement is the score of the new musical **RAGTIME** (based on the E.L. Doctorow novel, with book by Terrence McNally, produced by Livent, Inc.,) which was greeted with widespread critical acclaim at its world premiere in Toronto. A second company of **RAGTIME** premiered in Los Angeles at the Shubert Theatre in the Spring of '97, and the show arrives on Broadway in December of '97, where it will open the newly-renovated and restored Ford Center for the Performing Arts on the New 42nd Street.

Photo: JOAN MARCUS

Ahrens and Flaherty are the creators of the hit Broadway musical **ONCE ON THIS ISLAND,** which was awarded London's 1995 Olivier Award as Best Musical, and received eight Tony Award Nominations. NAACP Theatre Awards for Best Musical and Best Playwright, and Drama Critics Circle and Outer Critics Circle Nominations.

Also for Broadway, they wrote the score for **MY FAVORITE YEAR,** the first original American musical ever produced by Lincoln Center.

Their musical farce **LUCKY STIFF,** first produced off-Broadway by Playwrights Horizons, won the prestigious Richard Rodgers Award and subsequently Washington's 1990 Helen Hayes Award as Best Musical for its production at the Olney Theatre.

The team has recently completed the score for **ANASTASIA,** Twentieth Century Fox's first animated feature film (starring Meg Ryan, John Cusack, Angela Lansbury, Kelsey Grammer and Bernadette Peters) which will be released nationally in the Fall of '97.

Individually, Ms. Ahrens is the lyricist and co-book writer for **A CHRISTMAS CAROL,** New York's annual Christmas musical extravaganza at Madison Square Garden (with music by Alan Menken, choreography by Susan Stroman and co-book and direction by Mike Ockrent) which is entering its fourth holiday season. For her work in network television, Ms. Ahrens has received the Emmy Award and four Emmy nominations. Her songs are a mainstay of the renowned animated series **SCHOOLHOUSE ROCK,** and she created and produced such network shows as **DEAR ALEX AND ANNIE, H.E.L.P., THE DOUGHNUTS** and **WILLIE SURVIVE,** executive-produced the ABC Afterschool Special **THE UNFORGIVABLE SECRET,** and scored the Emmy-winning **STARSTRUCK,** as well as the feature film **A BILLION FOR BORIS.**

Mr. Flaherty wrote the incidental music for Neil Simon's new play **PROPOSALS,** scheduled to open on Broadway in the Fall of '97. He was also recently commissioned to write an orchestral suite based on the musical themes of **RAGTIME,** which premiered on the Fourth of July at the Hollywood Bowl, and his musical themes from **ANASTASIA** have been featured at the Bowl in a "Tribute to the Music of Twentieth Century Fox." He is a founding member of the new theatre company, "Drama Dept."

Cast recordings of their shows are available on RCA/Victor, Sony, Verese Saraband and TER and their music is published by Warner/Chappell Music. Both are members of the Dramatists Guild.

The "Ragtime" Creative Team

Left to Right: **Producer** Garth H. Drabinsky, **Choreographer** Graciela Daniele, **Composer** Stephen Flaherty, **Book Writer** Terrence McNally, **Original Novelist** E.L. Doctorow, **Lyricist** Lynn Ahrens, **Director** Frank Galati.

Ragtime

Lyrics by
LYNN AHRENS

Music by
STEPHEN FLAHERTY

Moderato (Not too quickly)

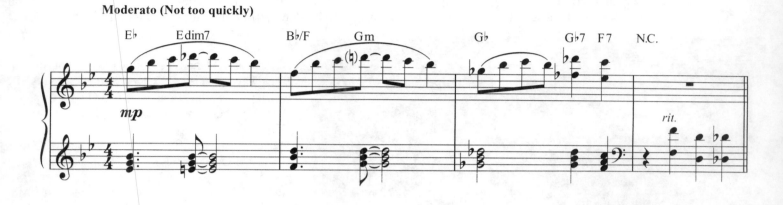

Ragtime - 8 - 1
PF9703

giv-ing the na - tion a new syn - co - pa - tion. The peo - ple called it Rag-time!

giv-ing the na - tion a new syn - co - pa - tion. The peo - ple called it Rag-time!

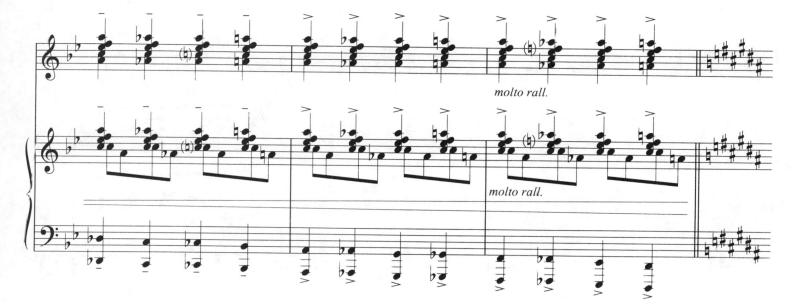

(Cakewalk)

WOMEN: And there was dis - tant mu - sic, skip-ping a beat, sing-ing a dream. La - la-la-la-

MEN: And there was dis - tant mu - sic, skip-ping a beat, sing-ing a dream.

Goodbye, My Love

Lyrics by
LYNN AHRENS

Music by
STEPHEN FLAHERTY

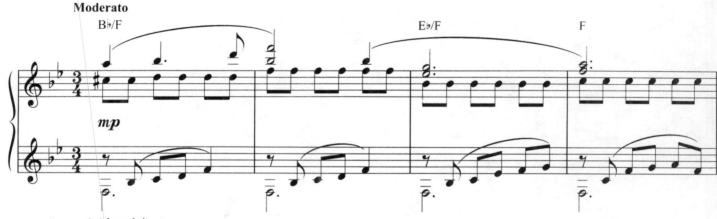

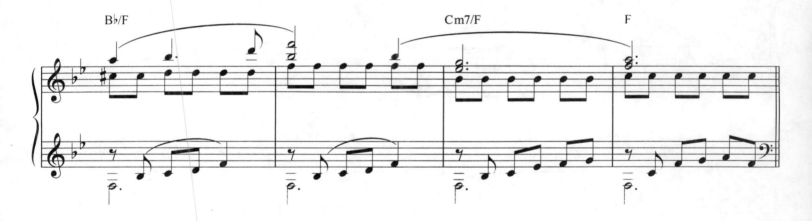

Good - bye, my love. God bless you.

Goodbye, My Love - 7 - 1
PF9703

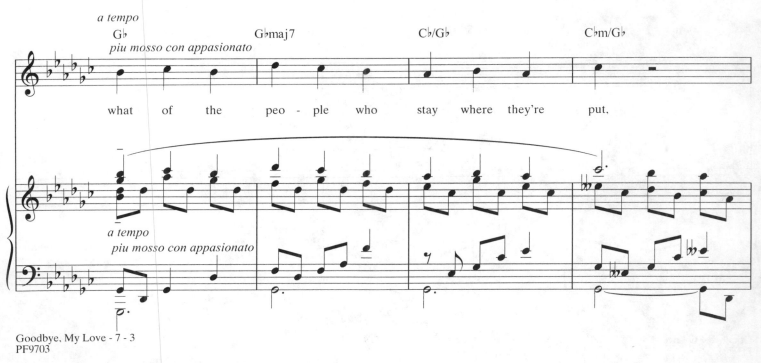

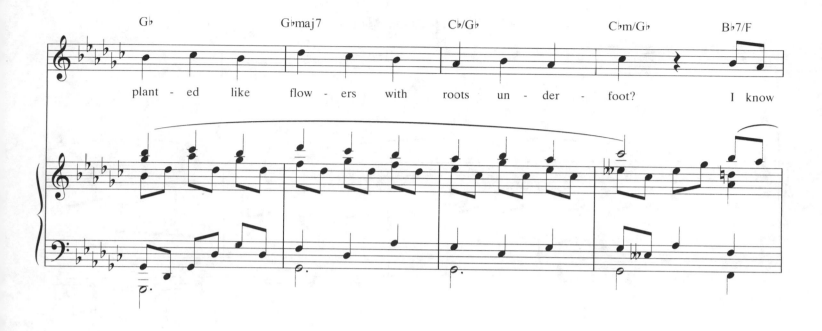

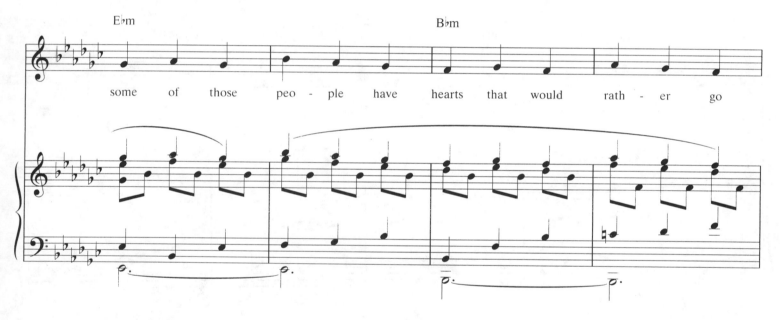

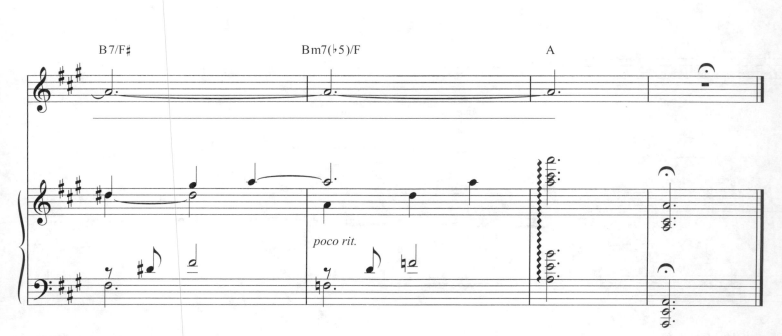

Your Daddy's Son

Lyrics by
LYNN AHRENS

Music by
STEPHEN FLAHERTY

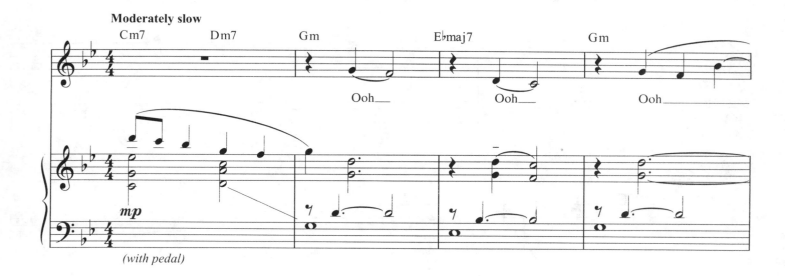

Your Daddy's Son - 5 - 1
PF9703

New Music

Lyrics by
LYNN AHRENS

Music by
STEPHEN FLAHERTY

F
Gm7
C7sus
C7
F
long?
MOTHER:
Just like that tune.
Gm7(♭5)/F
F
F/A
F7/A
B♭
N.C.
Gm7(♭5)/D♭
FATHER:
new mu - sic.
MOTHER:
sim - ple and clear.
I've come to hear new mu - sic.
MOTHER:
F/C
Gm7
C7
F
Why,
why can't you hear the song?

32

New Music - 11 - 3
PF9703

(NEIGHBORS+WORKERS:)

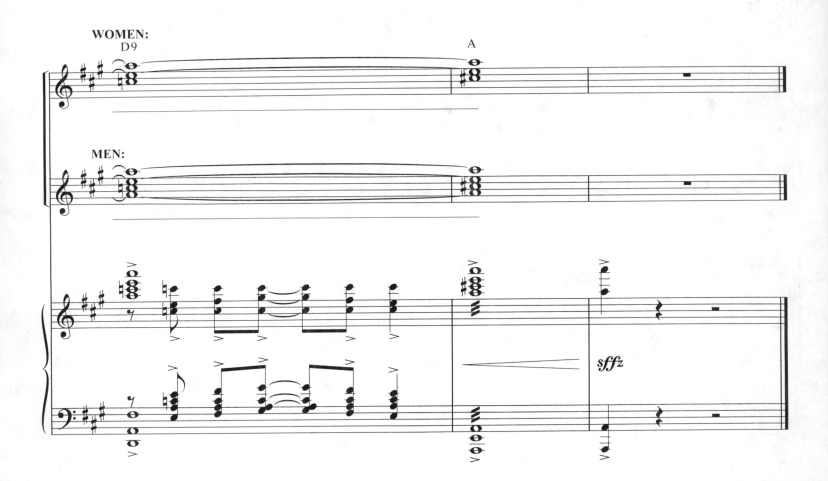

WHEELS OF A DREAM

Lyrics by
LYNN AHRENS

Music by
STEPHEN FLAHERTY

Wheels of a Dream - 10 - 1
PF9703

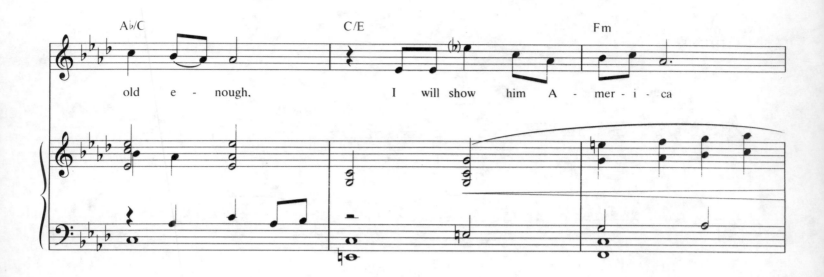

old e- nough,   I will show him A- mer-i- ca

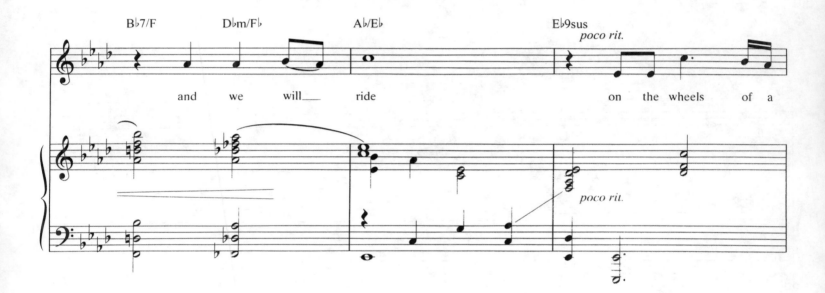

and we will___ ride   on the wheels of a

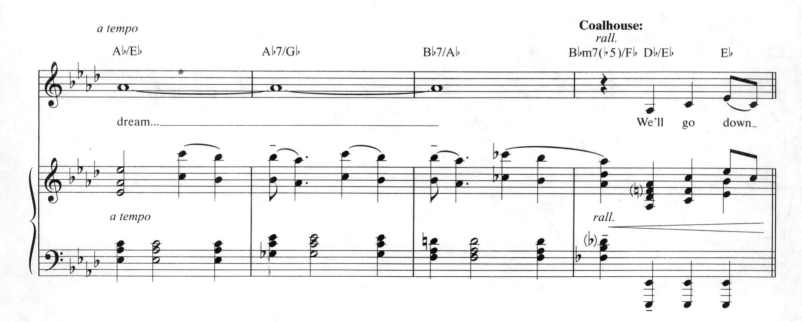

dream...___   We'll go down_

Coalhouse:

GLIDING

Lyrics by
LYNN AHRENS

Music by
STEPHEN FLAHERTY

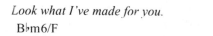

Gliding - 5 - 1
PF9703

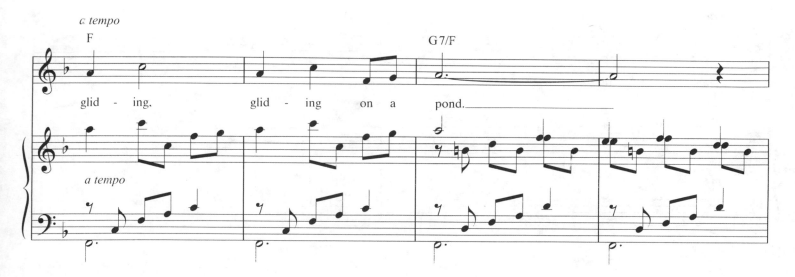

Feel ___ the wind as you pir-ou-ette. ___ Are you
hap-py yet? ___ Are you hap-py yet? ___
We are glid-ing, glid-ing far
a-way. ___ Pir-ou-ettes. Fig-ure eights.

'Till We Reach That Day

Lyrics by
LYNN AHRENS

Music by
STEPHEN FLAHERTY

'Till We Reach That Day - 10 - 1
PF9703

64

BUFFALO NICKEL PHOTOPLAY, INC.

Lyrics by
LYNN AHRENS

Music by
STEPHEN FLAHERTY

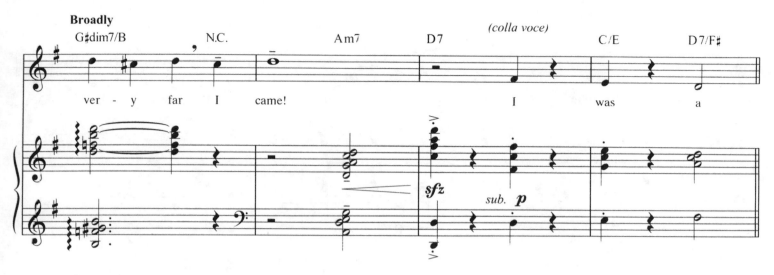

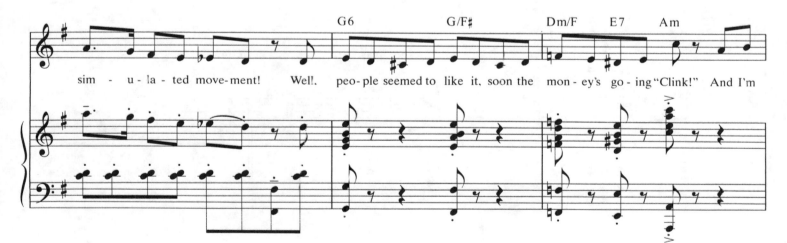

68

Lyrics:

sil - hou - ettes to pho - tos. I in - vent a small pro - jec - tor. And soon I'm mak - ing mov - ies and they're

cal - ling me di - rec - tor! An in - dus - try is dawn - ing and I'm stand - ing on the brink, Mis - ter

Buf - fa - lo Nick - el Pho - to - play, Inc.! Life shines_ from the

sha - dow screen!_ Com - i - cal, yet in - fi - nite - ly true.

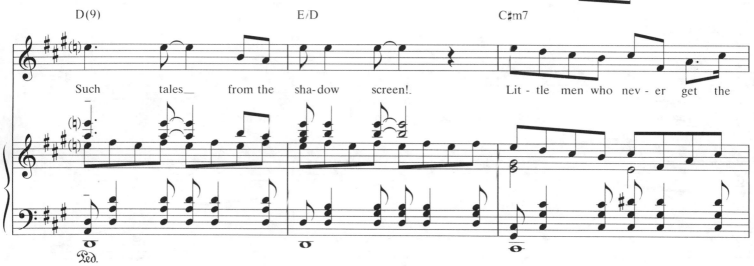

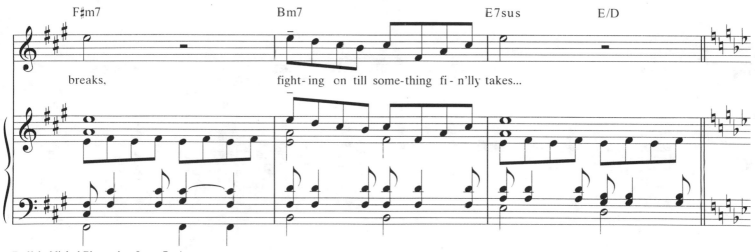

70

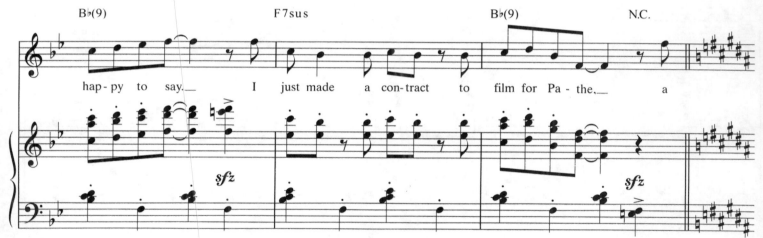

Buffalo Nickel Photoplay, Inc. - 7 - 5
PF9703

OUR CHILDREN

Lyrics by
LYNN AHRENS

Music by
STEPHEN FLAHERTY

Our Children - 6 - 1
PF9703

SARAH BROWN EYES

Lyrics by
LYNN AHRENS

Music by
STEPHEN FLAHERTY

Sarah Brown Eyes - 7 - 1
PF9703

Back To Before

Lyrics by
LYNN AHRENS

Music by
STEPHEN FLAHERTY

Moderately (in one)

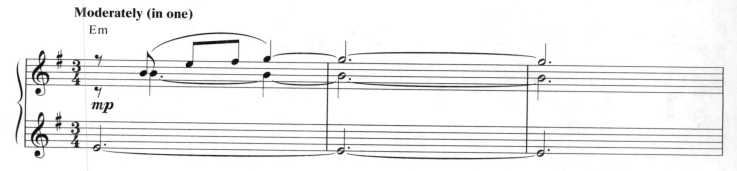

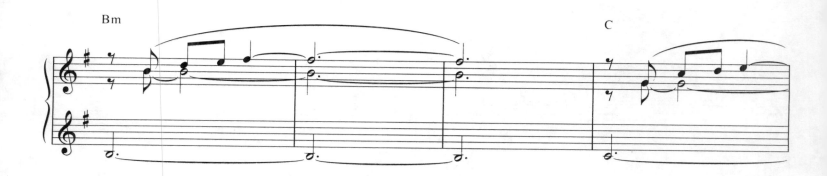

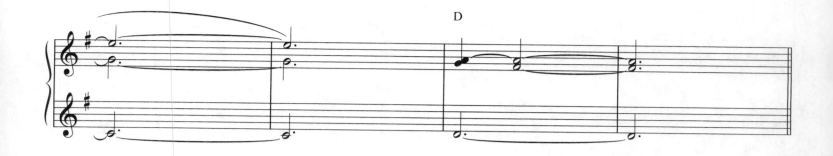

There was a time our hap-pi-ness seemed nev-er-

Back to Before - 13 - 1
PF9703

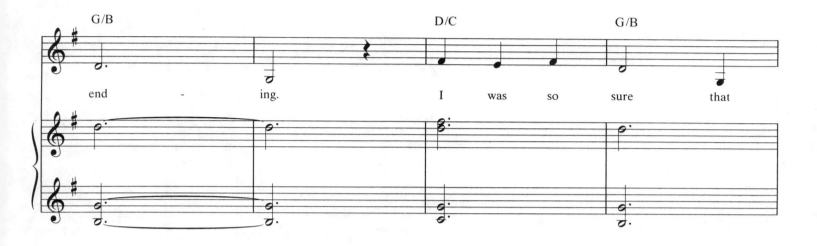

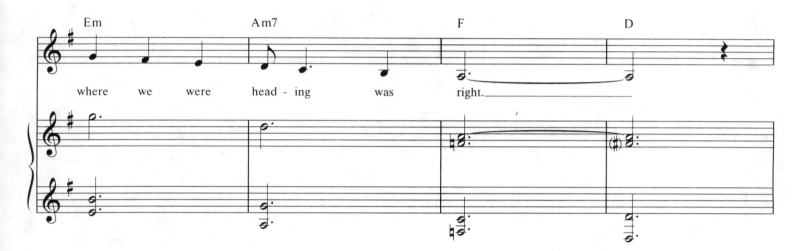

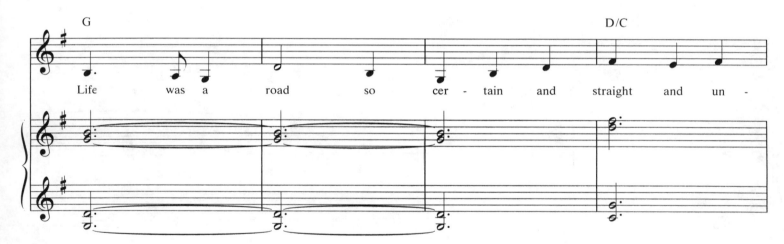

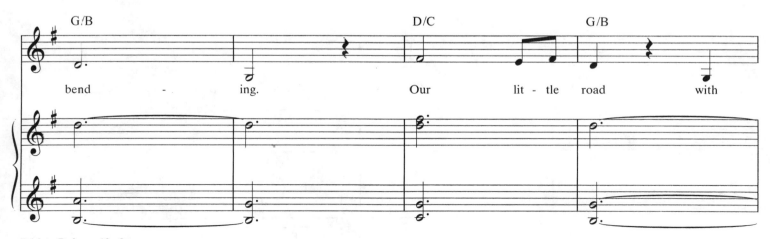

There was a time my feet were so sol - id - ly

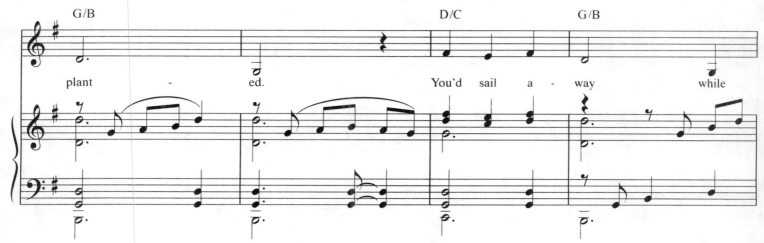

plant - ed. You'd sail a - way while

I turned my back to the sea._____

I was con - tent, a prin - cess a - sleep and en -

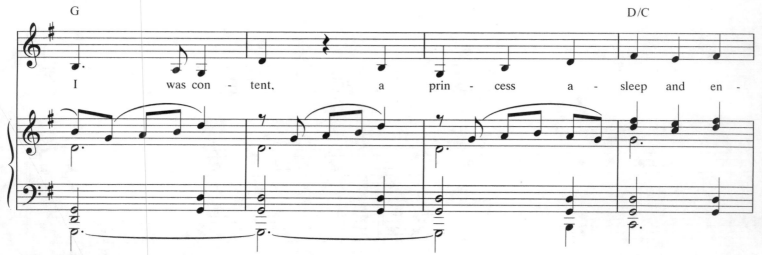

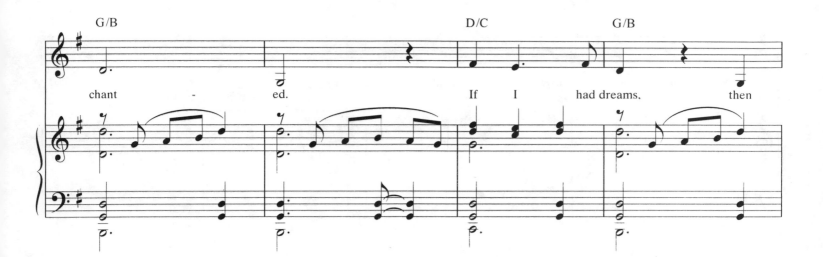

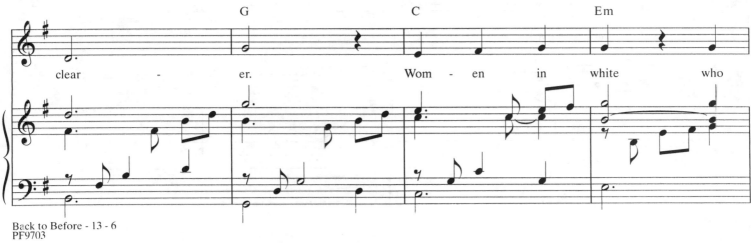

92

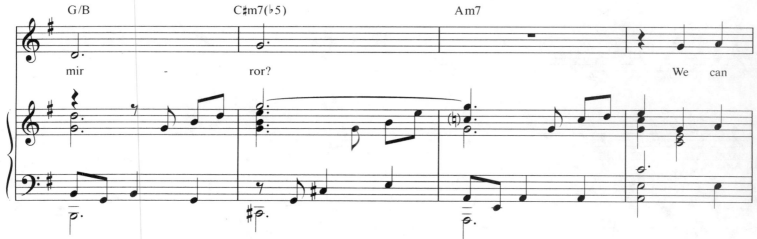

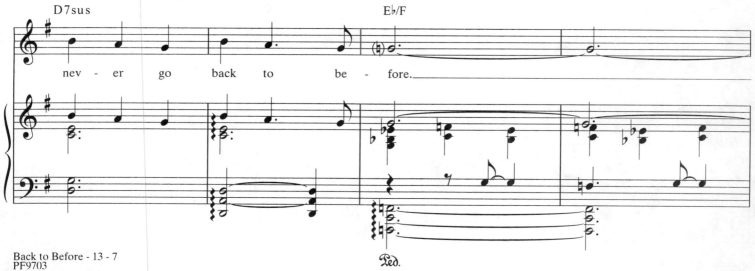

Back to Before - 13 - 7
PF9703

WOMEN:

There are peo-ple out there

un - a - fraid of re - veal - ing

Dm/F

94

I was your wife. It nev - er oc - curred to want

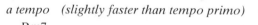

a little slower

more._____ You were my sky, my

mp *a little slower*

moon and my stars and my o - cean.

poco rit.

a tempo (slightly faster than tempo primo)

(roll down)

We can nev - er go back to be -

Back to Before - 13 - 12
PF9703

Make Them Hear You

Lyrics by
LYNN AHRENS

Music by
STEPHEN FLAHERTY